D1325486

WHIPPETS

For versatility and adaptability there are few dogs if any that can compare with the Whippet. Its handy size, affectionate nature, high intelligence, graceful proportions, hardiness and other attractive qualities have put this most lovable dog amongst the most popular of breeds. As a pet and companion the Whippet is clean, sensible and easily trained; out of doors he will race, catch rabbits, course hares and even retrieve. He is as keen a ratter as a terrier and as good a mouser as a cat. In this book Mr E. Fitch Daglish, the well known authority on dogs of all kinds, deals fully and practically with all aspects of general management, feeding, breeding and showing. There are also special chapters on the perplexing subject of colour breeding, and on Whippet racing and coursing which are now attracting new interest in many parts of the country.

WHIPPETS

E. FITCH DAGLISH

Revised by

MONICA BOGGIA

Edited by

ANNE MACDONALD

FOYLES HANDBOOKS
LONDON

ISBN 0 7071 0700 8

© *W. & G. Foyle Ltd. 1964*

Reprinted 1972
Revised edition 1980
Reprinted 1985
Reprinted 1986

Published in Great Britain by
W. & G. Foyle Ltd.,
125 Charing Cross Road,
London WC2H 0EB

Photoset and printed in Great Britain by
WBC Print Ltd., Bristol

CONTENTS

ILLUSTRATIONS

1

ORIGIN AND EARLY DAYS

THOUGH some details connected with the origin of the Whippet are obscure, there can be no doubt that the breed was made in England some time in the nineteenth century. Another fact of which we can be quite sure is that the Greyhound played an important part in its evolution, but there is some uncertainty as to which other breeds contributed to its genealogical history.

Origins of the breed
How this graceful little dog came to be known as the Whippet has never been satisfactorily explained. In the sixteenth century the word whippet was used as a general term for a small dog, but it became obsolete in later years and there is no evidence whatever that at the time our modern dog was being created that the word was generally known or used. Many years ago the Whippet was commonly referred to as the Snap Dog, the reason being, as one old-time writer states: 'Too fragile in his anatomy for fighting in the ordinary sense of the word, when molested he will snap at his opponent with such celerity as to take even the most watchful by surprise; while his strength of jaw, combined with its comparative great length, enables him to inflict severe punishment at the first grab.' Other authorities ascribed the title to the quickness with which the dog could grab or snap up a rabbit. Race Dog and Rag Hound are other names by which the Whippet was formerly known.

Many writers on the breed have asserted that originally the Italian Greyhound was crossed with the Greyhound to produce an animal similarly constructed but smaller than the larger hound. Although this theory has been repeated so often through the years that it has come to be regarded as a fact, it seems very unlikely. Just when the Whippet as we now know it was made is not exactly known, but it was probably somewhere about the 1850s. At that time the Italian Greyhound could not have been often seen in the mining districts of the north, which was the Whippet's original home, for it was then very little known anywhere in Britain. Furthermore, the few specimens which existed in this country in those days were very small—7 lb. or less in weight—and had neither the speed nor the sporting instinct which breeders wishing to produce a dog for rabbit coursing or racing might reasonably be expected to demand.

Writing of the Italian Greyhound in the 1860s Idstone stated that the number of good specimens to be found was very few and added, 'we have no hesitation in saying that it is the rarest dog of the day.' The suggestion that recourse was had to this rare breed to cross with the Greyhound for the purpose of producing the Whippet would appear, therefore, to be unjustified. It is much more probable that use was made of the smallest Greyhounds available—there were many coursers which did not exceed 30 to 40 lb. in weight—for crossing with various small, game terriers to reduce size and increase gameness and intelligence. Both smooth and broken coated breeds were probably used in different localities, for when Whippet racing was at the peak of its popularity in the north, rough-coated dogs were frequently seen on the tracks.

Whippet racing
Originally the Whippet was mainly used for rabbit coursing. The quarry was caught in nets, brought to an enclosed space where the trials were being held, and set free in front of a couple of dogs which were held by an official 'slipper' or handler. The rabbit was given a certain amount of 'law', usually about sixty yards, but had no chance of escape and must have been in a state of terror when let loose from the sack in which it had been confined. The winner was the dog which got to and snapped up the rabbit first.

When criticism of the cruelty involved in this barbarous pastime caused it to be discontinued, attention was turned to racing Whippets along a straight track. Speed then became of paramount importance. The competitors were handicapped according to size. There was a wide margin of difference in the weight of the dogs entered, but it soon became evident that the middle size, round about 17 lb., was the best for racing, though some of the most successful performers were considerably smaller, and a dog named Moley Rat, considered to be one of the fastest of all time, turned the scale at over 26 lb.

The distance covered in a race was generally 200 yards, though this was sometimes increased, and a good dog was expected to run 200 yards in slightly under 12 seconds. The *modus operandi* followed was for each dog to be held on its mark by a slipper, who grasped his charge firmly by the scruff of the neck with the right hand and by the base of the tail with the left, at the same time raising the dog's hind-quarters well above the ground. On the discharge of the starter's pistol each slipper swung his dog forwards and threw him as far as possible in such a way that he alighted on his feet, thus getting off to a flying start. The owner or trainer stationed himself a little beyond the winning line waving a towel or strong rag of some kind and calling his dog, which had been trained to race to rag, as it was termed. On passing the winning line each competitor hurled itself at the towel being waved by its trainer, seizing it and hanging on with such tenacity that the momentum of its arrival caused it to be swung high in the air. The dogs were usually raced on cinder tracks, which were straight and level, though occasionally grass covered tracks were used.

Equality of opportunity
The fact that bitches were faster than dogs was taken into consideration in handicapping, a dog being allowed two and a half to three yards advantage for every pound difference in weight between it and a competitor of the opposite sex. An article by Theo. Marples, written about 1895, gives some details of the method of handicapping. A weight of 15 lb. was taken as the basis of the handicap, each dog being allowed three yards for every pound by which it varied from this. But when the dogs reached about 27 lb. in weight they were pretty much equalized, just as an increase was given to small dogs down to about 8 lb. in weight. For instance a dog of 15 lb. would give one of 14 lb. three yards start; but one of 13 lb. would receive seven yards from a 15 lb. dog, and in all likelihood a 10 lb. dog would receive from 18 to 20 yards in the two hundred. Then, in turn, the 15 lb. dog would receive three

yards from the 16 lb. animal, and from one up to 20 lb. the 15 lb. dog would receive from 10 to 12 yards start. Novices were usually given an advantage of about 2 lb.

The centre of rag racing was Lancashire, two of the most famous tracks having been at Oldham and Bury, where at the turn of the century upwards of 300 dogs were not infrequently entered in one handicap.

The Whippet was popular in the colliery areas of the north east long before it made its debut as a show dog, which did not occur until the last decade of the nineteenth century. The early exhibits were not specially bred for show purposes but were picked up from dogs which had been trained for racing but had failed to display sufficient merit to get among the winners. At that time fanciers who were aware of the successes that had been achieved in the show ring by other breeds soon saw the possibilities of popularising a good-looking Whippet in competitions in which the exhibits were judged entirely on appearance, and were always ready to pay the comparatively small prices asked for symmetrically constructed dogs that had proved unfit for racing. It was these discards, many of them of unknown pedigree, which became the ancestors of the show Whippet as we know it today.

Official recognition

The breed was not officially recognized until 1890, when the Kennel Club acceded to a petition submitted by Herbert Viccars, who was one of the most enthusiastic of the early exhibitors. The Whippet Club was formed in 1899 for the purpose of fostering the best interests of the Whippet as a show dog. Prior to that date the only bodies working for the breed were concerned solely with rag racing.

Among the pioneers of the Show Whippet Mr. F. H. Bottomley was, perhaps, the most prominent. He began showing early in the 1890s and his prefix Manorley quickly became famous. Another most successful kennel was that owned by Mr. Albert Lamotte, whose prefix Shirley will always be of special significance in the history of the development of the modern Whippet. Over the last three quarters of a century many great Whippets have appeared but practically all trace back to Ch. Shirley Wanderer and his son

Ch. Manorley Maori. These two may be regarded as having been pillars of the breed in the truest sense. Photographs of these two great sires, as well as those depicting other early exhibits bearing the Shirley and Manorley prefixes, afford conclusive proof of how little type has changed through the years. Judging from their portraits, such old-time celebrities as Champions Shirley Wanderer, Shirley Siren, Shirley Lorna, Manorley Maori, Manorley Mode and the lovely Manorley Moireen would give a good account of themselves in our rings today in competition with our best contemporary winners, though it is probably true to say that in 1957 (when this book was originally written) there were more first class Show Whippets than at any time before or since.

2

THE WHIPPET AS A COMPANION

AS EXPLAINED in the previous chapter, the Whippet was originally evolved by the miners and mill workers of the industrial north to meet the requirements of the more humble of the sport-loving fraternity in the sphere of rabbit coursing and rag racing. In those days no importance was attached to the dog's actual appearance; its sole value lay in its speed and agility. But an animal in which swiftness and gameness were the qualities most desired had to be sound, and grace and elegance came as inevitable concomitants, though no efforts were made to cultivate them. The growth of interest in dog shows naturally brought new interest in the breed from those who recognized it as a likely subject for ring competition, and the best looking specimens that could be found at the race tracks were eagerly sought for by would-be exhibitors. This soon led to the Whippet becoming known in parts of Britain in which it had hitherto rarely, if ever, been seen, and the show-going section of the dog-loving public gradually became familiar with a breed which till then had only been known by name, if at all, as the Race Dog.

For long the breed remained in the hands of a comparatively small number of enthusiasts, however, and its potentialities as a family dog and companion remained unsuspected by the great majority of dog lovers. So little was the dog really known and understood that less than sixty years ago even some of those who were regarded as authorities on matters canine, while expressing admiration for its physical symmetry, found it difficult to say anything in praise of its companionable qualities. This mistaken attitude was, doubtless, largely responsible for the Whippet staying among the outsiders, or minor breeds, so far as the owners of family pets were concerned. Its failure to attract wider support was also fostered by the popular error that it was unsuitable for life as a household companion, not only because of special requirements in the matter of feeding and exercise, but because of its naturally delicate constitution, which necessitated great care in protecting it against cold.

As a show dog the Whippet continued to make steady progress and to attract wider support, but through the first quarter of the present century the breed never won general recognition as a particularly desirable family companion. It is, indeed, only comparatively recently that its merits have been generally appreciated and the Whippet has risen to its present very well-deserved position among the top twenty of Britain's most popular dogs. It must certainly be a source of great satisfaction that this charming and exquisitely beautiful little dog is winning its way into the hearts and homes of an ever increasing number of our countrymen.

Whippets as pets

Now that the breed has become known to so many people, there is every reason to believe that it will attract more and more adherents as time goes on, for this most lovable dog has many virtues and no drawbacks. As a pet it is intensely affectionate, very easily trained, highly intelligent, exceptionally clean in the house and easy to manage and keep in health. Its sleek coat does not harbour dust or vermin and requires the minimum attention in the way of grooming; its small, neat feet do not bring in mud or dirt; its small size and gracefulness are perfectly suited to the modern home. Its appetite is small, so that it is not difficult or expensive to cater for, and the breed is very hardy, so that it is not likely to develop any of the hereditary diseases or defects which often cause distress in some other breeds.

In addition, the Whippet is one of the most adaptable and versatile of dogs. It is unexcelled as a rabbiter, will course hares, is as efficient and eager at ratting as any terrier, and is as good a mouser as a cat. As a race dog it stands alone, can be taught to find game and to retrieve, and of recent years has surprised many of its admirers by taking top honours at Obedience Tests. In short, there is no field of activity appropriate to a dog of its size in which a Whippet cannot shine.

In the home the Whippet's needs are few and simple. He loves

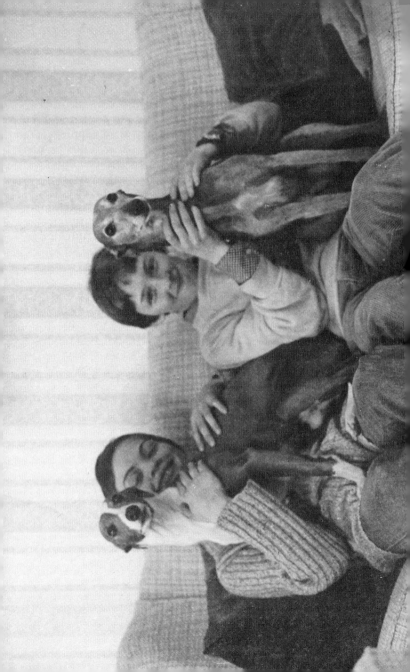

warmth, human companionship, comfort and a place to which he may retire to sleep and rest, and which he will come to regard as especially his own. The old idea that the Rag Hound lived in solitude away from canine companions in an isolated kennel and came in contact with its owner or handler only when actually racing or training, is wholly fallacious. As soon as a puppy was old enough to begin training it was taken into the house, where it was usually ensconced in the family kitchen. It played indoors throughout the day, was taken for a road walk when its master returned from work in the pits or mills and, more often than not, slept in the children's bed. Thus from its earliest days the breed has been reared as part of its owner's family, and the modern Whippet still enjoys being part of a family and settles down naturally and happily in any home in which he can share the life and love of the inmates.

Whippets need warmth
Though perfectly hardy and a real sporting dog, the Whippet is sensitive to cold—especially to cold winds or draughts. Indoors a coat is not normally necessary, but a bed placed in a sheltered position and furnished with one or two soft, warm blankets in which the dog may keep warm and snug is an essential require-ment. The shape of the bed is immaterial, provided it is of suitable size, but it should be raised well above the level of the floor in order to be out of the way of all draughts, and provided with a good solid front and sides, six inches or so in depth, to give additional protection. A good-size covered box with an entrance aperture in one of the sides is very suitable. Even a large cardboard carton with a good size hole cut in one side may be made to serve. This may be considered somewhat unorthodox, but it has the advan-tage that it may be destroyed and replaced frequently, so that the need for cleaning and disinfecting at intervals is eliminated.

While enjoying brisk exercise out of doors a coat is not usually necessary, except in very cold weather, but if the dog is taken for a sedate walk or exercised in conditions which involve slow movement or frequent stops, as when out shopping, a coat should

Opposite: Whippets make lovable pets—especially for children

be provided. It is impossible to lay down any hard and fast rule as regards Whippet clothing. The only satisfactory way is to consult the dog's comfort and if in any doubt on the matter to rug him up, the coat used varying in weight with the season. Apart from keeping out the cold wind, a rug is likely to have a very beneficial effect on the natural coat. If unprotected a dog will grow a thicker, harsher and somewhat longer coat in winter than in summer, but by making judicious use of a rug the coat may be kept looking short and sleek throughout the year.

Exercise

Many people have been put off keeping a Whippet as a pet by the idea that a dog of this breed needs more exercise to keep fit than, for example, a terrier or other dog of similar size. This belief is quite without foundation. A Whippet can be kept in perfect health, if properly fed and housed, with the amount of exercise necessary for any other kind of sporting dog. The minimum requirement may be considered to be from half to three-quarters of an hour brisk road walking each day with, when possible, opportunity to enjoy romping or unrestricted gambolling in a garden, park, field or other open space for about the same time. The Whippet is very active and playful, so that he may be depended on to take as much exercise as possible throughout his waking hours either in the house or outdoors, but he has the very useful trait of curling up in a small space out of the way when desired to do so.

Don't be in too great a hurry to get a puppy on to road walking on a lead. As a rule it is safe to start road work at the age of six months. By then the feet, shoulders and quarters may be expected to be sufficiently strong to stand up to this form of controlled exercise without harm. Much will, however, depend on the stage of development reached by the individual puppy. Some dogs take much longer to firm up in body than others, and until the bones are hard and the joints well-knit, road walking should not be begun. Until that stage has been reached a puppy should get all the exercise he needs by romping and playing, with opportunities to

Opposite: The ideal waterproof coat for a Whippet (Photo: Anne Cumbers).

rest quietly immediately he tires. The importance of regular road work, and the vital role it can play in producing and preserving soundness in a show Whippet, is dealt with at length in a later chapter.

Feeding

The feeding of a Whippet kept as a family dog presents no special difficulty. The two most important principles to observe are: always use plain, natural foods and never overfeed. A fat dog of any breed is never really healthy and a fat Whippet is an abomination! The ideal is for a Whippet to show their ribs. For an adult two meals per day are usualy ample. These may be offered at any times to suit the convenience of the owner, but it is important that the feeds are given regularly, at the same times each day.

Meat and wholemeal rusks or biscuits should form the mainstay of the diet, with eggs, fish, offal and full-cream milk offered, perhaps once a week, as a change. This should provide all the nutrient and vitamins essential to ensure robust health.

The only deficiency that may arise is in regard to vitamins of the B series, which form a complex group. Some of them are present in small quantities in the foods mentioned and others are normally synthesized by bacteria inhabiting the intestines. In some dogs, however, this gut flora seems at times to fail and a deficiency of one or more of the B vitamins gives rise to symptoms of ill-health. The richest natural source of vitamins of the B group is brewers' yeast, and the addition of this substance, most conveniently given as yeast tablets, is a wise precaution. These tablets improve both appetite and digestion, as well as having a beneficial effect on the skin and coat.

Most Whippets do well on a light meal in the morning and a more substantial one in the evening, but it is impossible to be dogmatic about how many meals an adult dog should have. A good deal depends on the appetite and the nutritional needs of the individual, as well as on age and condition. The dog's digestive organs are adapted to dealing with fairly substantial meals eaten at widely separated times, so that, except in special cases, the number

Opposite: A game of tug-of-war with an old fur collar.

of feeds per day should not exceed two. What matters much more than the number of meals, or the hours at which they are given, is regularity in feeding times. A dog is largely a creature of habit and will respond much more satisfactorily to a feeding routine to which he has become accustomed than to the same amount and quality of food offered at different times from day to day. Strict attention to regularity in feeding times should be started as soon as a puppy begins to take solid food and continue throughout the dog's life, though the number of feeds necessary will vary at different ages (see Chapter 8). A full meal should never be given before a spell of violent exercise or immediately after a period of great exertion. If a dog comes home overtired or exhausted, he should be left to rest for at least an hour before being given a heavy meal.

Never leave uneaten food standing about. Stale food is a fertile source of infection, besides which the sight of food constantly before it is more likely than almost anything else to spoil a dog's appetite and make him a finicky feeder and a bad doer. The amount of food needed each day will vary greatly from one Whippet to another. It depends, among other things, on age, the amount of exercise taken, size and individual idiosyncrasy. As a very rough guide it is suggested that about three quarters of an ounce be allowed for each pound the dog weighs, and of this two thirds should be meat or its equivalent in protein value. Starchy foods (carbohydrates) should not be fed too liberally, otherwise the dog will probably put on surplus flesh or fat and lose its sparkle and verve. A raw marrow bone will give great enjoyment and is a very useful means of keeping the teeth strong and white. Detailed instructions for feeding growing stock of all ages is given in Chapter 8.

3

GROOMING AND ROUTINE MANAGEMENT

THE SHORT, fine coat of the Whippet requires much less attention than does the thicker, longer covering of many other dogs, but grooming must not, for that reason, be neglected or considered unimportant. Daily grooming will not only ensure that the coat and skin are kept free from dust, dirt and external parasites but, if properly performed, will stimulate the skin, encourage cutaneous circulation and keep the muscles supple. Kneading, massage and hand slapping are among the best of all conditioners and will impart a healthy gloss to a sleek coat more surely than will the application of any patent dressing or skin lotion. Hand rubbing or massage will bring about a wonderful improvement in a bad doer which always seems to lack flesh over the spine, or in a dog that is soft in muscle after an illness or period of enforced inactivity. By this means weight may be put on an animal which no amount of food seems to fatten. The old stableman's saying that a thorough grooming is as good as a feed is as applicable to a Whippet as to a horse.

A vigorous daily grooming will also help to fine down a dog that is on the fat side, for by stimulating the skin and underlying muscles it produces a feeling of well-being and thereby encourages activity.

The appliances required for grooming a Whippet are few and simple. All that is necessary is a small dandy brush, a bristle brush in which the bristles are not too hard and of medium length, or a brush in which rubber spikes take the place of the usual bristles, a hound glove, and a soft cloth or leather for finishing off and putting on the final polish. When grooming it may be found convenient to stand the dog on a table or raised surface of some kind, so that all parts of the body can be easily reached and thoroughly dealt with.

21

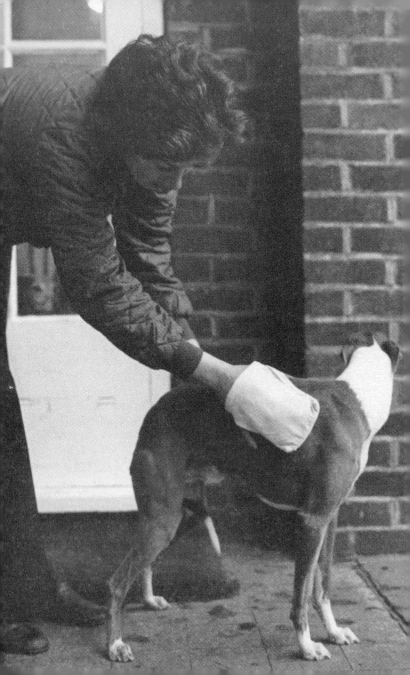

Eyes

At grooming time the dog is brought under close inspection and any slight sign of ill-health, like a dry nose, dull or discharging eye, or a tendency to roach the back and shiver, may be spotted. A dog's eyes are a pretty reliable guide as to its general health. In a really fit animal the eye is clear, bright and free from discharge. A dull, inflamed or weeping eye should always be viewed with suspicion.

An eye discharge may be caused by mechanical irritation set up by a fragment of grit or other solid particle. It may be due to a cold in the eye or to conjunctivitis following bacterial infection. All discharge should be removed with a swab of cotton wool soaked in boric lotion and applied at blood heat. Open the eye gently and bathe, or depress the lower lid and flood the eye with a few drops of the lotion. Warm castor oil dropped in the eye is soothing and is the safest means of removing a piece of grit or a grass seed that tends to adhere to the eye-ball. Any discharge that has dried on the lids should be removed, vaseline being used to soften crusts before applying the lotion.

When the eyes are inflamed, a little golden eye ointment smeared on the inner edges of the lids, and the eyes closed till it has diffused over the eye-balls, will hasten recovery. Should the eyes continue to discharge and irritation be indicated by the dog rubbing its paws over the organs, the cornea may be injured, in which case the wisest course is to obtain veterinary advice.

Nose

Nasal discharge should be removed at once, using a mild antiseptic, or the dog's head may be held over a jug of steaming water to which friar's balsam or eucalyptus has been added—about a spoonful to a quart. A clear, watery discharge from the nostrils may be of little significance, but if it is thick or yellowish a deep-seated malaise may be indicated. Dry crusts should be carefully removed and the nostrils be kept clear by frequent swabbings. A dry nose is usually regarded as a sign that all is not well, but if there is no rise in temperature there is not much cause

Opposite: Grooming with a hound glove.

for worry. In some dogs the nose seems to be permanently dry after a febrile illness. The condition may be alleviated by periodic treatment with vaseline.

Ears
Ears should be looked at daily and as a preventative measure a little canker powder may be dusted or gently blown into them once a week. The ear flaps must be kept clean. If necessary they may be wiped with soap and water to remove any dirt or dried food particles that may be adhering to them, then carefully dried and their inner sides lightly smeared with olive oil.

Nails
The condition of the nails or claws should be checked periodically. Given a well-formed foot with correctly arched toes, the nails should be kept short if the dog is sufficiently exercised on hard ground. But if the pads are soft or the toes flat, the claws will not be worn down but grow too long, causing the toes to spread and, possibly, bringing the dog down in its pasterns. Even if the foot is of the correct shape and construction, circumstances may arise which cause the nails to become overgrown and it may be difficult to rectify matters.

The longer a nail grows the further down the quick will penetrate, and a stage is eventually reached when shortening the claw becomes an operation calling for expert veterinary super-vision. This trouble may be avoided by keeping the nails short throughout a dog's life from early puppyhood. In a young puppy the quick is quite short and the nails may be clipped or rasped back quickly, easily and safely. Thereafter the claws should be kept worn down by road work, or prevented from becoming long by having a little removed with a clipper or a coarse file whenever it is necessary.

In hot weather tar can be a menace to dogs exercised on roads, especially in the country. Tar is difficult to remove once it has set hard and may cause painful or irritating sores if picked up on a

Opposite: Care of the nails is important and these clippers are easy to use; take care though and watch an expert first.

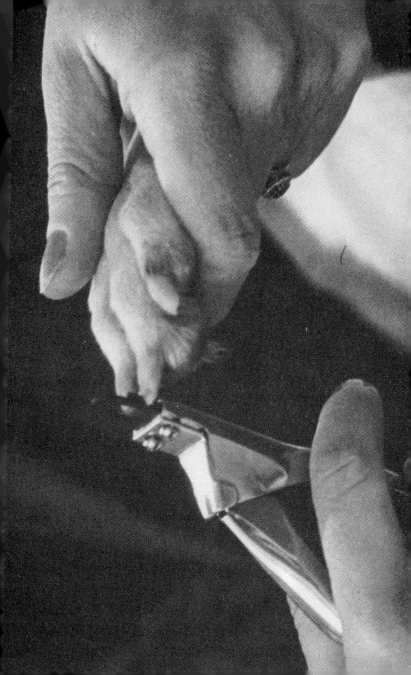

dog's feet. Every possible effort should be made to prevent a dog walking over soft tar but if, despite all precautions, this substance adheres to the pads, or to the hair between the toes, it should be removed as soon as possible by rubbing with lard or other soft fat. If this is not done dust, dirt or grit will be picked up and may give rise to purulent swellings.

Teeth
If a dog is properly fed its teeth should give little trouble. But a dog fed wholly on soft food may have the teeth disfigured by accretions of tartar. This discolouration may sometimes be seen on a dog which has plenty of bones and other hard tack included in its diet, but that is unusual. If the deposit is not removed from time to time the teeth may fall out or have to be drawn. Any tooth which shows tartar discolouration should be scaled, using one of the special scrapers sold for the purpose. After the first scaling it may be necessary to repeat the treatment at intervals of six months.

If dealt with before the teeth are badly affected, tartar need cause no dental injury, but if neglected the gums may become inflamed and recede from the base of the teeth, completely spoiling the appearance of the mouth and causing offensive breath. Rubbing the teeth with diluted hydrogen peroxide or a powder dentifrice will keep the teeth of a pet dog white and its mouth sweet.

General care and management
One of the advantages the Whippet has over many other breeds is that it requires neither stripping nor trimming to keep it presentable or in show condition. Straightforward grooming is all that is necessary to ensure that the dog always looks smart, clean and ready to take its place in the show ring without special preparation. At the most, a little tidying up may be needed by individuals in which the hair on the sides of the neck, behind the thighs or on the underside of the tail, tends to grow too long or thick, so that it detracts from the sleekness of the general outline. Too thick a growth on the sides of the neck may be thinned either by judicious hand plucking or by means of special thinning scissors. Excessive

Opposite: Correct bite or dentition.

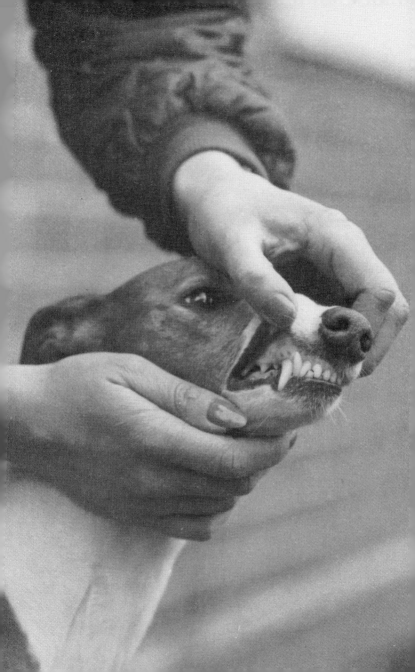

length of the hair on the backs of the limbs and under the tail may be cut back, great care being taken not to attempt too much or to leave the coat looking uneven or ragged.

In a book of this size it is clearly impossible to deal in detail with the diseases that may afflict a dog. The Whippet is naturally hardy and if comfortably housed, well fed and sensibly treated, is rarely ill. Any dog that shows the slightest symptom of being out-of-sorts should have a temperature check. The normal temperature is about 101·5°F (38·5°C). Should it rise a degree or more above that the dog should be isolated and kept quiet in a warm place until a veterinary surgeon can make a detailed examination. In the initial stages of some diseases the temperature of the body may fluctuate widely and frequently, so that where sickness is suspected a dog's temperature should be taken several times over a period of twelve hours. A single thermometer reading cannot always be accepted as a reliable guide to an animal's condition.

4

THE IDEAL CONFORMATION

SOON AFTER its inception in 1899 the Whippet Club drew up a Standard of Points by which the breed was to be judged in the show ring. The ideal aimed at was a Greyhound in miniature, so there was no great difficulty in defining the qualities required, so far as anatomical construction was concerned. The first Standard did, in fact, follow very closely that relating to the Greyhound except, of course, in the clause concerning size, in which the desired weight was given as 20 lb. Today the Whippet is judged by what is virtually the same Standard, though in the course of the years that have elapsed since it was originally issued a few amendments and additions have been made to render the description of the ideal clearer and more complete.

The ideal
The modern version of the Standard of Points runs:

General appearance. Should convey an impression of beautifully balanced muscular power and strength combined with great elegance and grace of outline. Symmetry of outline, muscular development and powerful gait are the main considerations; the dog being built for speed and work, all forms of exaggeration should be avoided. The dog should possess great freedom of action; the forelegs should be thrown forwards and low over the ground like a thoroughbred horse, not in a hackney-like action. Hind legs should come well under the body giving great propelling power; general movement not to look stilted, high stepping, short or mincing.
Head and skull. Long and lean, flat on the top tapering to the muzzle, rather wide between the eyes, the jaws powerful and clean cut; nose black, but in blues a bluish colour is permitted and in

livers a nose of the same colour. In whites and parti-colour a butterfly nose is permissible.

Eyes. Bright, fairly round, not too small and full of expression.

Ears. Rose shaped, small and fine in texture; folded back in repose and raised when alert, but never pricked.

Mouth. Level. The teeth in the top jaw fitting closely over the teeth in the lower jaw.

Neck. Long and muscular; elegantly arched.

Forequarters. Shoulders oblique and muscular, the blades carried up to the spine and closely set together at the top. Forelegs straight and upright, front not too wide, pasterns strong with slight spring, elbows set well under the body.

Body. Chest very deep and plenty of heart room, brisket deep and well defined, back broad, firm, somewhat long and showing definite arch over the loin but not humped, loin giving the impression of strength and power, ribs well sprung; well muscled on the back.

Hindquarters. Strong and broad across the thighs, stifles well bent, hocks well let down, second thighs strong, the dog then being able to stand over a lot of ground and show great driving power.

Feet. Very neat, well split up between the toes, knuckles highly arched, pads thick and strong.

Tail. No feathering. Long, tapering; when in action carried in a delicate curve upward, not hooked or ringed or carried over back.

Coat. Fine, short, as close as possible in texture.

Colour. Any colour or mixture of colours.

Size. The ideal height for dogs is $18\frac{1}{2}$ inches and for bitches $17\frac{1}{2}$ inches, although many of today's winners are well over the desired size.

Faults

Under *Faults* the following defects are specially mentioned:

Front and shoulders. Weak, sloping or too straight pasterns, pigeon toes, tied elbows, loaded or bossy shoulders wide on top, straight shoulder blades, flat sides. An exaggerated narrow front not to be encouraged.

Head and skull. Apple skull, short foreface or down face. Ears pricked or tulip. Mouth over- or under-shot.

Neck. Throatiness at the join of neck and jaw and at base of neck.

Body and hindquarters. A short coupled or cramped stance, also an exaggerated arch, a camel or humped back (the arch starting behind the shoulder-blades) a short or over long loin. Straight stifles, poor muscular development of thighs and second thighs.

Feet. Splayed, flat or open.

Tail. Gay, ringed or twisted, short or docked.

Coat. Wire or broken coated; a coarse or woolly coat; coarse thick skin.

All-round quality

If read carefully this description should convey to anyone of ordinary intelligence a clear picture of what is required in a typical Show Whippet and what are the principal faults to avoid. The first impression it should make on the mind of the reader is that the Whippet is essentially a small, smooth-coated, sporting dog possessing great speed, a very lively mentality, with exquisite elegance, grace and agility. Its Greyhound ancestry is plainly shown in its general build and conformation, while the terrier blood which went into its making is indicated by its gameness, quick intelligence and adaptability.

All-round quality is probably higher today than at any previous time in the breed's history. So much so, that in a well-filled class at any of the larger shows the judge's job of sorting out the winners is anything but a sinecure and calls for a real appreciation of the finer points. Often there is no great gap between the exhibit placed first and many of those which have to be relegated to the losers' end of the line. In the Whippet ring what may be termed jig-saw judging is completely out of place. By that is meant that it is quite contrary to the spirit of the Standard to try to assess a dog's value by considering the degree of excellence shown by its separate parts, such as the head, front, backline, quarters, feet and so on, in isolation. Excellence in a Whippet depends principally on balance and symmetry, and on the way in which the shape and proportion of the various parts combine to fit the animal to perform the job of racing and running-down and catching small, fleet-footed quarry.

Much less importance is attached to the details of head structure than is the case with many other breeds, in which, unfortunately, it is apt to influence a judge's placings more than body conformation or even soundness. But though of less fundamental significance than body, legs and feet, a badly shaped or wrongly proportioned head can greatly mar the expression and general appearance of an otherwise good exhibit. The skull should be flat between the ears and sufficiently wide to provide adequate room for the brain of a dog of the Whippet's high intelligence. A narrow, domed skull is grossly untypical. The eyes should be of medium size, well set, bright and sparkling. If too small or deep set they give the dog a sulky expression, whereas if too large and round the outlook is too mild and dull. Both skull and foreface should be clean cut and of moderate length, with strong jaws and level bite. This is necessary to enable the dog to reach and grip a fast-moving prey. A short, weak or too shallow muzzle is the reverse of what is wanted. Both an underhung and a pig jaw are very serious faults.

A long, well-muscled, supple neck is needed in a dog used for coursing, so that he may grab and pick up his fast-moving and quick-turning quarry in flight. The neck should be gracefully arched at the nape and run cleanly into the junction with the breast in front and into the well laid back shoulders behind.

Great depth is a characteristic of a good Whippet. In an animal in which speed and stamina are essential qualities, heart and lung room are of supreme importance, and these depend on depth of chest rather than on the width of the ribbing. The thorax, or rib-cage, must be well-developed and extend well back. The length of this portion of the body can be judged by the underline, which should be well-defined and form an unbroken curve from the brisket to near the fore edge of the pelvis. A short thorax gives an abrupt break in the underline at the termination of the ribbing, and makes for weakness in the region of the loin.

The back must be well-padded with muscle on both sides of the spine, and the top-line should run cleanly from the withers, with a graceful and not too accentuated arch, over the loins. This line is very important. The correct conformation is well shown in the dogs and bitches whose photographs are reproduced in our illustrations. Years ago a roach or wheel back was a commonplace; the top-line being more or less strongly arched from the withers to the fall away at the croup. In those days many exhibitors seem to have been unaware that a wheel back was a fault, for the exaggerated arch was often made more conspicuous by the way in which the exhibits were made to stand, and it is up to today's judges to ensure this fault does not return.

Ears are apt to be ignored but, though they are of little moment in comparison with some other points, there can be no denying that correctly shaped and carried ears aid greatly in imparting the true Whippet expression. Today the prick or tulip ear, once very frequently seen in the breed, is largely a thing of the past, though still occasionally noticed in our rings. Large, thick textured ears are, however, far from uncommon. The ideal is the small rose-shaped ear, normally carried folded back but brought forward and half pricked when the dog's attention is aroused.

The forelegs must be rather long and perfectly straight and parallel. The elbows should be so placed that the points are quite flat and close to the surface of the thorax, turning neither in nor out, and when the dog moves the joints should move freely to give a long, low stride. The points of the elbows should be level with, or slightly below, the deepest point of the chest. Though the front should not be broad, it must not be too narrow or close, or the front action will be cramped and as this fault often goes with straight, that is insufficiently sprung, ribs, a narrow fronted animal may appear slab sided. The pastern is the area between the wrist and the toes and should be of good length, strong but flexible, so that when standing it inclines slightly forwards from the perpendicular. A short, perfectly vertical pastern like that of a Terrier is quite wrong in a Whippet.

The feet are an important feature in any running animal. This is generally recognized, both by breeders and judges. Really bad feet are not often seen today. The main thing is that the pads must be tough, hard and resilient, the toes long and close, each well-formed and well-arched. In general shape the foot should be oval, but the so-called cat foot with short toes, which is so much admired in certain terrier breeds, is not correct. It is, indeed, as far removed from the typical Whippet foot as is the flat-toed, oblong hare foot.

B

The coat is characteristic. It should be short, fine and carry a natural gloss, the muscles rippling beneath it with every movement the dog makes. There is sometimes a tendency for the coat to be somewhat longer and coarser than it should be, particularly on the tail. This may be corrected to some extent by grooming and judicious trimming, but basically the trouble is genetic and can be permanently overcome by careful selective breeding.

Size

Size is one of the subjects most often discussed by Whippet enthusiasts. In some circles it is felt that many, perhaps the majority, of the dogs winning in the ring are too big and that to correct this trend in the breed a maximum height should be imposed and incorporated in the Standard. Others feel that that would be a retrograde step and cause too much importance to be attached to mere size at the expense of general type and structure. Though it must be conceded that the Whippet is essentially a small dog, it would seem most undesirable to try to stabilize size in the breed at a definite level. The existing Standard mentions $18\frac{1}{2}$ inches for dogs and $17\frac{1}{2}$ inches for bitches as ideal heights but makes no attempt to lay down either a maximum or a minimum height, leaving it to judges to use their discretion as to the extent to which variation from the ideal should be penalized. This attitude would appear to be realistic and sensible. What it means is that if two exhibits are equal in all respects save size, the one which approaches most closely the ideal height for its sex should have the verdict, but that type, balance and symmetry should be considered as of greater value than actual height, provided the general breed stature is retained and that the dog does not resemble a Toy on the one hand or a Greyhound on the other. There has always been a good deal of variation in size in the Whippet from the time of the old Rag Dog from which he descends. This is clear from the handicapping charts of the 1890s, which refer to animals ranging from as little as 9 lb. to those weighing upwards of 30 lb.

In the United States Standard the ideal height for dogs is given as from 19 to 22 inches and for bitches as between 18 and 21 inches, but, again, it is stressed that these are not intended to be taken as fixing exact size limits.

Shoulders and hindquarters have still to be considered. Both have much to do with movement and the details of their structure is of sufficient significance in determining correct action fore and aft as to warrant a separate chapter being devoted to them.

5

STRUCTURE AND MOVEMENT

IN THE paragraph devoted to forequarters the Standard states that the shoulders should be oblique. This refers to the setting of the scapula or shoulder blade, which is the bone on the size, shape and angulation of which correct movement in front largely depends. If the shoulder is to be well laid back, as it should be, the scapula must be long and slanting, so that its broad upper end is laid against the vertebrae of the spine as far back as possible. At its lower end the shoulder blade should join the upper part of the humerus, or bone of the upper arm, at an angle of about ninety degrees. The humerus should also be long, and so set that its lower end articulates with the bones of the foreleg at the elbow at the angle required to bring the legs well under the dog in line with the deepest part of the chest. If the scapula is too short the shoulder cannot be right. A short shoulder blade, instead of sloping well back from the point where it meets the humerus to the withers, will be too upright, so that its upper end is brought forwards towards the base of the neck and the lower and upper arm bones meet at an angle considerably greater than ninety degrees. This will have the effect of bringing the whole shoulder girdle too far forward. It also predisposes towards loose elbows and general unsoundness in front. If the shoulder blade is correctly placed, the interplay between the several joints of the forequarters enables the con-cussion caused by such violent exercise as jumping, leaping and galloping over rough ground, to be absorbed without any undue strain being inflicted on any part of the forequarters.

With a long, broad, obliquely set scapula the muscles covering it will be distributed over a considerable area, so that the shoulder will be close-lying, clean and well defined; whereas with a short scapula the muscles on both sides of the bone will tend to bunch, causing the shoulder to stand out from the body. This completely spoils the flat, sleek outline, which contributes so much to that look of grace and elegance without which the Whippet loses so much of its charm.

There is usually a close relationship between the length of the scapula and that of the humerus. If one is short the other is short too. Thus, upright shoulders are generally associated not only with lumpy muscle on the region of the shoulder blade but also with a similar lumpiness in the area overlying the upper arm. It is this condition that produces the fault referred to as loaded shoulders, the basic cause being short, upright shoulder blades.

As already mentioned, in a dog with upright shoulders the upper end of the scapula is brought forward towards the base of the neck. This makes the neck look short and badly set. Instead of the neck line running cleanly and gracefully into the shoulders, it tends to meet the back line at an abrupt angle, further accentuating the appearance of heaviness in front. Upright shoulders are almost always accompanied by a short, stuffy neck and there is often a tendency for the front to be unduly wide. Faulty shoulder placement also has an adverse effect on fore action. A dog with upright shoulders will have a restricted or stilted gait. He cannot move with the long, low stride which carries the feet well in front of the body, as asked for in the Standard.

Hindquarters

Turning now to the hindquarters, correct action here depends mainly on the setting or slope of the pelvis, which affects the position of the hip joints, and on the proportionate length of the bones of the upper and lower thighs and the angle formed by them at the stifle. The propelling power of the hindquarters is derived partly from this angulation and partly from the musculature of the loin, pelvis and the upper and lower thighs. If the angulation at the stifle is insufficient, a dog cannot possess the backward thrust or propulsion necessary to enable it to gallop for long periods without becoming exhausted, or to jump and leap with ease and agility. But correct angulation is not all that is required. To be effective this must be accompanied by strong muscular development on both the upper and lower thighs. Only when these parts are well-muscled can hind action be really strong, forceful and co-ordinated. But if the second thigh is to be well-muscled without being clumsy, it must be of good length, which means that the hock must be low. What is wanted is length from hip to hock, with well bent stifles and hock joints. Hocks are sometimes too high. This detracts from the length and drive of the stride, tending to produce a mincing gait behind.

Show critiques often refer to the fault of going close behind. This applies to a dog which, though he may appear satisfactory when standing, in moving brings the hind legs so close together that he seems to be unbalanced and weak in quarters. This may result from the limbs being loosely articulated at the hip, from a too narrow pelvis, or from the long bones of the legs being slightly incurved, so that in action they converge from hip or stifle to hock.

The head of the femur or thigh bone fits into the socket in the pelvis called the ascetabulum, the whole joint being enclosed in a tough, fibrous capsule. The position assumed by the shaft of the femur depends largely, therefore, on the angle it makes with this joint. If the angle is too small the thigh bone on either side of the body will tend to incline inwards, whereas if the angle at the hip joint is too wide the bones will diverge towards their lower ends, causing the lower legs to be unduly wide apart, so that the dog may be faulted for going too wide behind. An unsteady gait may be caused by looseness at the hip joint, which throws the point of the stifle outwards when the dog is moved at a brisk pace. This condition often goes with cow hocks, in which the hock joints are inturned and the feet inclined outwards. This is a very bad and extremely ugly fault. For perfect hind action the limbs must be moved absolutely straight and parallel throughout their length, with strong flexion at the stifle and hock, and with sufficient space between the moving limbs to give a firm, steady stride and an appearance of balance to all the other parts of the body.

The value of road exercise

Though many of the physical failings which cause bad action may be genetic in origin or produced by faulty rearing or indifferent housing, it is probable that insufficient attention to the needs of a Whippet in the matter of exercise is responsible for much of the

Opposite: Road walking.

defective action so often seen. Many exhibitors fail fully to appreciate the value of road walking for building up and preserving sound movements. A daily spell at a brisk pace will do much to prevent the appearance of action faults stemming from non-congenital causes and to greatly improve existing ones. Loose elbows which do not come from faulty bone structure are often caused by soft or undeveloped pectoral muscles. In a good fronted dog these muscles brace the elbows firmly to the sides of the thorax. If they are feeble or flabby the whole shoulder becomes sloppy and fore action is ruined. The best remedy is hard road work. A dog that is regularly exercised in this way rarely fails in front movement unless there is something radically wrong with its anatomical formation. The same results cannot be produced by exercising on soft ground or by galloping. Too much romping or running at speed over grass may, indeed, produce faulty shoulders and elbows, especially in young dogs.

Reference has previously been made to the part incorrect angulation or proportional length in the bones of the hind legs may play in making for unsoundness behind, but unless the bones on either side of the stifle carry sufficient muscle of the right thickness, breadth and length, and the loins are strong, the full propelling force on which positive effective action depends will not be available and movement is bound to be poor and will deteriorate as the dog tires. Road exercise will build up the muscles of these parts more quickly and satisfactorily than any other treatment. It will also strengthen the hocks and make for strong flexion in the stifle and hock joints.

Galloping uphill in moderation is also useful in developing muscle on the quarters and helps to give breadth behind, and free running is valuable both for its physical and mental effects. But running at liberty or hunting in fields cannot give the results that can be secured by road work in bringing and keeping a dog on its toes and in maintaining or improving hind movement. Action is sometimes made to look unbalanced by soft, open or splayed feet or by weak pasterns. However well-shaped a dog's natural feet may be, the maintenance of the correct conformation depends on the pedal muscles, tendons and ligaments being kept firm and strongly contractile. If allowed to get slack or weak the toes will lose their arch and become straight, so that the whole foot looks wrong. This deterioration is aggravated by soft pads, for in the absence of a firm support the foot soon opens and spreads. Here, again, road work provides the best and only certain remedy. Once these faults have developed no amount of exercise on soft ground will effect much improvement. Weak pasterns, too, may be greatly improved by regular exercise on hard roads, though it may take time, perhaps several months, to obtain the results desired. If matters have been long neglected the ligaments may have become stretched and inert. It may then be difficult, if not impossible, wholly to correct the trouble, but even in such cases some measure of improvement may generally be achieved.

6

SHOWING AND HANDLING

Watching the Whippets being judged at a big show, the beginner can hardly fail to notice the different ways in which the exhibits are presented for judicial examination. Some stand anyhow, with their backs humped and legs all over the place, or so restless or uneasy while in the ring that they are constantly on the move, so that it is well-nigh impossible to get a good view of their outline. Others seem always to be standing well, assuming a pose which sets them off to the best advantage and appear to be quite unperturbed by their surroundings. A ringside spectator may suppose that the quiet, well posed dogs are owned and handled by professionals or by very experienced exhibitors, and that to train a dog to show in this way needs a long apprenticeship and an almost inexhaustible fund of patience. Such a supposition is totally wrong. There is, in fact, nothing at all difficult in training a Whippet to show itself off in the approved manner; neither is this training beyond the power of the youngest novice.

Natural showers?
There are a few dogs which may be said to be natural showers. They seem to enjoy being the centre of attraction and appear to know instinctively just how to make the most of themselves, automatically taking up a becoming attitude immediately they realize they are being looked at. Such individuals are, however, few and far between in any breed. The majority of dogs need training in show deportment before they make their debut in ring competition; but that does not involve anything difficult or complicated. All the most exacting judge requires is that an exhibit brought before him shall stand still for a minute or two in a position in which its qualities may be assessed, move in a certain direction in a straight line when required to do so, and to submit quietly to such manual examination as may be deemed necessary.

42

An exhibit which refuses to stand still or which persistently assumes an unbecoming attitude and when moved hunches its back, hangs its head, slinks along, gambols wildly or tries to interfere with other competitors, is almost sure to be passed over, for it is virtually unjudgeable.

Show training

Before starting on a show career a Whippet should be taught to take and hold a pose in which its general make and shape is favourably displayed, and to move in a straight line at a pace that suits it best, going freely but collectedly on a slack lead. The sooner training begins the better. Preliminary instruction may be started when a puppy is three months old. At that age youngsters are very impressionable, quick at learning, if treated with gentleness and patience, and have retentive memories. The periods of instruction must at first be short, but the more frequent they are the better results will be.

When posing the pupil see that the forelegs are well under the body, absolutely straight and parallel, with the feet pointing straight to the front. The hindlegs must be so placed that the stifles are nicely bent and the hocks perpendicular, parallel and well separated. If the fore and hindlegs are correctly placed the top line and body are almost sure to be right, but be careful that the back is not too much extended, but gracefully arched over the loin without being too much roached. The head should be held high enough to show off the length of the neck, but not tilted upwards or too far back, as this will spoil the general balance and symmetry and make the dog look ewe-necked. At first it will be difficult to persuade the puppy to stand in the position desired, but patience and perseverence will be rewarded. It is surprising how quickly even a very young puppy will settle down and co-operate if it is spoken to quietly and encouraged. Never let handling degenerate into anything resembling a struggle. This will inevitably scare the pupil and cause it to be obstinate and seem stupid.

The next step is to get the puppy to hold the desired pose when your hands are removed. If it immediately moves or sits down, as it is very likely to do, quietly place it in position again and each time it is reposed repeat the word 'Stand'. Do not expect too much at first, but if the lesson is repeated for a few minutes once or twice daily most puppies will learn to retain the pose for half a minute or so in a week or ten days. The ultimate aim is to teach the youngster to take up the required pose on the command 'Stand' without being touched, though minor corrections to the stance may be necessary for a time. Later the puppy must be taught to walk quietly on a lead and to move freely in any direction indicated, but that is very easy to do once initial training in road walking has been given. For the show ring it is essential to find your dog's best natural pace to show off the best movement possible.

A dog cannot be expected to behave well in public unless it has become used to being among strange people and other dogs. As soon as a puppy has been inoculated it should have opportunities of mixing with the owner's friends and visitors. An occasional trip to a shopping centre will do much to overcome early nervousness. Given a chance to adapt itself to the conditions in which it is destined to live, a puppy will grow up obedient and friendly, with neither fear nor suspicion of the unfamiliar. More often than not bad showmanship is due to lack of proper show training.

Health
Before taking a dog to a show be sure he is perfectly fit. Remember that at a show he will probably be exposed to a greater concentration of infection than he normally experiences and if he is at all below par he will be much more likely to contract an illness than he would if at the top of his form. If a dog is even slightly off colour he cannot be expected to show at his best. Prior to setting out, therefore, make a final check and if there is any doubt about the dog's fitness don't take him.

Coat
If a dog is to have a reasonable chance of success he must be put down in perfect bloom. This condition cannot be obtained by starting a course of special show preparation a few days before the date of a show. It comes from careful attention to feeding,

Opposite: Mr Terry Thorn judging a Whippet class at Malvern (Photo: Anne Cumbers).

exercising, grooming and general kennel hygiene. Cleanliness is, of course, essential; the coat should be shining and immaculate. If regularly groomed a coloured Whippet will rarely need to be washed, but in the case of a white or particolour a bath may be considered advisable. If so it should be given two or three days before the event, otherwise the coat may look dull and somewhat rough. Use a good soap or dog shampoo; detergents are very likely to irritate the skin and either bring out a rash or cause the dog to scratch. Damping slightly with rain water before grooming and hand massage will help to put a gloss on the coat. A final polish with a piece of silk will add the professional touch.

In the ring

When getting a Whippet into position in the ring, first see that both the fore- and hindquarters are correctly placed, with the front legs perpendicular, not too far apart and quite parallel and the hindlegs well but not too much bent at the stifles, the hocks vertical and fairly widely separated. See that the dog is standing comfortably and that the back-line shows a nice arch over the loin. If it is necessary to handle an exhibit, do not make the common mistake of placing a hand under the loin and holding it up. This will probably have the effect of exaggerating the arch and make the back appear to be roached. A hand under the jaw may help to bring the head up and slightly forward, but do not cover the muzzle with the hand. This not only detracts from the dog's expression but makes it impossible for the judge to make a fair assessment of the proportions of the head. Above all do not raise the muzzle too high, so that the nose points upwards. This will have the effect of pushing the head back and make the line of the neck too upright, spoiling the clean, graceful junction with the line of the back at the withers. It may also impart a convex outline to the throat which, though typical in the Italian Greyhound, is wrong in the Whippet, in which the neck should be held slightly forward and the throat line be straight or very slightly concave, as may be seen in the dogs portrayed in our illustrations.

After the show

On arriving back home after a show, it is a wise precaution to sponge the dog over with a mild disinfectant, paying special attention to the eyes, nose, mouth and feet, and to check his temperature daily for a week, so that if any infection has been picked up it may be dealt with immediately the first symptoms appear.

7

BREEDING

SUCCESS in breeding Whippets depends a good deal on the quality of the brood bitch, and it should be realized that certain physical properties other than show points are necessary.

The breeding background

A prospective brood should possess such basic attributes as good bone, adequate depth and width of ribbing, plenty of room in the pelvic region and a sound constitution. A narrow, short or constricted pelvis is to be avoided. It is most desirable to check on the bitch's reproductive background; that is, to ascertain that she comes from female forebears that were good whelpers and satisfactory mothers. The unfortunate tendency to ignore the need to retain constitutional soundness, normality and fecundity—while concentrating too exclusively on trying to produce animals possessing a high degree of excellence as regards visual show points—has been largely responsible for many of the hereditary shortcomings which now affect some breeds. Happily, up to the present, the Whippet has remained free from such defects. Breeders should do all in their power to keep things this way by remembering, when arranging matings, that such qualities as fertility and the ability to whelp naturally and rear the puppies satisfactorily are just as important as are show points.

Breeding Whippets is a fascinating undertaking in which there is always something yet to be learnt and in which there is bound to be some element of chance. Perhaps the best advice that can be offered to the beginner is: don't expect success to come without working and planning for it. Don't leave anything to chance if you can avoid it. Learn all you can about the blood lines which have produced the leading winners in the breed. Study pedigrees and try to understand the principles on which successful breeding is based. Let each mating made be the outcome of careful thought, observation and study.

Nouakula Whippets

Colour photos by Anne Cumbers

Nouakula Nobleman

*Whippet brindle : Nouakula
Noble Star*

*Cock Crow Sirios in his coat :
owned by Mrs. Baker*

Whippets are good with children

Nouakula Night Knight : 16 months old

Walking dogs before a Whippet race

The start of a Whippet race

Mating

A Whippet bitch may come in season for the first time at any age between six and twelve months of age. The onset of heat is normally indicated by a vaginal discharge, which is at first colourless but after a few days becomes reddish. This lasts for about a week, when the show of colour ceases and the period of true heat supervenes. This phase continues for about seven days, but its duration may be either considerably shorter or longer. It is only during true oestrus that the bitch is eager to mate or when a mating is likely to be fruitful. The best time to put a bitch to a dog is usually from the tenth to the twelfth day after the first signs of her coming in season appear. At this time the vulva will be swollen and soft, and the bitch will encourage the attentions of the male.

No hard-and-fast rule can be given regarding the age at which a Whippet bitch should first be bred from, since so much depends on the individual and the state of her development. Some bitches are ready at a year old but others are better left for another six months. It is certainly most undesirable to breed from a bitch before her skeletal growth is completed. Until she is sufficiently mature her body is in no fit state to stand up to the strain of bearing and rearing a family. If bred from too soon her litter is likely to be either small or weakly and her own growth will be arrested, in addition to which she may be spoilt for future breeding.

A bitch should not be fed for two hours prior to being mated. If taken to a stud dog at a distance she should be rested for a short time and exercised before being introduced to her prospective mate. If the bitch is a maiden and the dog has difficulty in effecting penetration, the vagina may be lightly lubricated with a little vaseline or liquid paraffin. Only a slight smear is necessary. If too much is used it may act as a contraceptive. During the tie both animals should be firmly held in a comfortable position and kept under control until release occurs naturally. On the completion of mating the bitch should be allowed to rest quietly for half an hour or so and offered a drink before being taken home.

Feeding

Whippet bitches usually whelp easily and require only reasonable care and treatment during the period of pregnancy. The idea that to ensure a full litter of healthy puppies and to safeguard the dam against undue strain it is necessary to increase her food intake immediately after she has been mated, is quite mistaken. Such a course is, in fact, most inadvisable. If the bitch is in good, hard condition her usual feeding routine should be continued for the first four weeks of pregnancy. In the early stages the nourishing of her embryo family imposes no considerable strain on her and the amount of food she consumes has no direct influence either on the number or the rate of growth of her foetal puppies. She should be able to supply all the nourishment required on her usual rations without loss of condition.

The rational method of feeding a bitch after she has been mated is to keep her on her ordinary diet until the fifth week, when she may begin to show signs of being in whelp, and then to gradually increase her meals by additional meat, eggs or fish, as her appetite increases. But it is most important to see that a small dose of halibut-liver oil and some absorbable calcium, such as calcium gluconate or prepared bonemeal, is given daily to maintain the requisite amounts of minerals and vitamins A and D in the blood. The theory that the inclusion of supplementary minerals and vitamins in the diet of the bitch throughout pregnancy is likely to cause the puppies to be so large at birth as to make whelping difficult, may be dismissed as groundless. To produce strong, well-developed, lusty whelps with a high degree of resistance to infection the dam's calcium-phosphorous and vitamin intake must be increased.

The golden rule to remember is: don't be tempted to overfeed during the first month of pregnancy, but be sure not to underfeed, especially as regards proteins and minerals, during the last three weeks. If a bitch is given more food than is required to repair her own tissue wastage and nourish her unborn young she will put on surplus flesh or fat—a condition which is to be avoided at all costs, for obesity is one of the most common causes of whelping difficulties. The best way to help a bitch to whelp normally and easily is to keep her active, hard and muscular. As her time approaches and her figure broadens it is, of course, necessary to see that she does not risk injury by indulging in rough play or foolhardy antics, such as jumping from a height or trying to

GESTATION TABLE

Showing when your bitch is due to whelp

MATED JANUARY	DUE TO WHELP MARCH	MATED FEBRUARY	DUE TO WHELP APRIL	MATED MARCH	DUE TO WHELP MAY	MATED APRIL	DUE TO WHELP JUNE	MATED MAY	DUE TO WHELP JULY	MATED JUNE	DUE TO WHELP AUGUST	MATED JULY	DUE TO WHELP SEPTEMBER	MATED AUGUST	DUE TO WHELP OCTOBER	MATED SEPTEMBER	DUE TO WHELP NOVEMBER	MATED OCTOBER	DUE TO WHELP DECEMBER	MATED NOVEMBER	DUE TO WHELP JANUARY	MATED DECEMBER	DUE TO WHELP FEBRUARY
1	5	1	5	1	3	1	3	1	3	1	3	1	2	1	3	1	3	1	3	1	3	1	2
2	6	2	6	2	4	2	4	2	4	2	4	2	3	2	4	2	4	2	4	2	4	2	3
3	7	3	7	3	5	3	5	3	5	3	5	3	4	3	5	3	5	3	5	3	5	3	4
4	8	4	8	4	6	4	6	4	6	4	6	4	5	4	6	4	6	4	6	4	6	4	5
5	9	5	9	5	7	5	7	5	7	5	7	5	6	5	7	5	7	5	7	5	7	5	6
6	10	6	10	6	8	6	8	6	8	6	8	6	7	6	8	6	8	6	8	6	8	6	7
7	11	7	11	7	9	7	9	7	9	7	9	7	8	7	9	7	9	7	9	7	9	7	8
8	12	8	12	8	10	8	10	8	10	8	10	8	9	8	10	8	10	8	10	8	10	8	9
9	13	9	13	9	11	9	11	9	11	9	11	9	10	9	11	9	11	9	11	9	11	9	10
10	14	10	14	10	12	10	12	10	12	10	12	10	11	10	12	10	12	10	12	10	12	10	11
11	15	11	15	11	13	11	13	11	13	11	13	11	12	11	13	11	13	11	13	11	13	11	12
12	16	12	16	12	14	12	14	12	14	12	14	12	13	12	14	12	14	12	14	12	14	12	13
13	17	13	17	13	15	13	15	13	15	13	15	13	14	13	15	13	15	13	15	13	15	13	14
14	18	14	18	14	16	14	16	14	16	14	16	14	15	14	16	14	16	14	16	14	16	14	15
15	19	15	19	15	17	15	17	15	17	15	17	15	16	15	17	15	17	15	17	15	17	15	16
16	20	16	20	16	18	16	18	16	18	16	18	16	17	16	18	16	18	16	18	16	18	16	17
17	21	17	21	17	19	17	19	17	19	17	19	17	18	17	19	17	19	17	19	17	19	17	18
18	22	18	22	18	20	18	20	18	20	18	20	18	19	18	20	18	20	18	20	18	20	18	19
19	23	19	23	19	21	19	21	19	21	19	21	19	20	19	21	19	21	19	21	19	21	19	20
20	24	20	24	20	22	20	22	20	22	20	22	20	21	20	22	20	22	20	22	20	22	20	21
21	25	21	25	21	23	21	23	21	23	21	23	21	22	21	23	21	23	21	23	21	23	21	22
22	26	22	26	22	24	22	24	22	24	22	24	22	23	22	24	22	24	22	24	22	24	22	23
23	27	23	27	23	25	23	25	23	25	23	25	23	24	23	25	23	25	23	25	23	25	23	24
24	28	24	28	24	26	24	26	24	26	24	26	24	25	24	26	24	26	24	26	24	26	24	25
25	29	25	29	25	27	25	27	25	27	25	27	25	26	25	27	25	27	25	27	25	27	25	26
26	30	26	30	26	28	26	28	26	28	26	28	26	27	26	28	26	28	26	28	26	28	26	27
27	31	27	1 (May)	27	29	27	29	27	29	27	29	27	28	27	29	27	29	27	29	27	29	27	28
28	1 (Apl)	28	2	28	30	28	30	28	30	28	30	28	29	28	30	28	30	28	30	28	30	28	1 (Mar)
29	2	29	3	29	31	29	1 (July)	29	31	29	31	29	30	29	31	29	1 (Dec)	29	31	29	31	29	2
30	3	—	—	30	1 (June)	30	2	30	1 (Aug)	30	1 (Sept)	30	1 (Oct)	30	1 (Nov)	30	2	30	1 (Jan)	30	1 (Feb)	30	3
31	4	—	—	31	2	—	—	31	2	—	—	31	2	31	2	—	—	31	2	—	—	31	4

squeeze through spaces too narrow for her, but controlled exercise should be encouraged right up to the last.

Whelping

The bitch should be introduced to the box or kennel in which she is to whelp about a fortnight before she is due. This will ensure that she becomes familiar with her whelping quarters and that she will not panic or make frantic efforts to get back to the place where she has been accustomed to sleep at the critical moment, as she may otherwise do. The whelping box or chamber should be warm, secluded and comfortable. It should be large enough to allow her to lie stretched out at full length and to turn easily. A flange of wood or a rail fixed round the sides, just below the level of her back when she is lying down, will prevent the risk of the new born puppies being overlaid or inadvertently injured by the mother. For whelping the box may be covered with several thicknesses of newspaper or sheets of corrugated cardboard. If preferred it may be furnished with a mattress made of sacking or similar strong material stuffed, not too tightly, with fine woodwool. Loose straw, hay or coarse woodwool should never be used. The first two are almost sure to harbour vermin, while the last is likely to irritate the skin of the mother and to be injurious to very young puppies.

The whelping quarters must be absolutely dry and draught proof. In the house artificial heating may be unnecessary, but in an outside kennel or in cold weather some means of maintaining an even temperature of 70°F (21°C), or a little above, is most desirable. The portable dull-emitter infra-red lamps now available at low cost are very satisfactory if used as directed by the makers' instructions.

The normal period of gestation is sixty-three days, but puppies may be born at any time between the fifty-eighth and sixty-sixth day. Shortly before parturition starts a bitch usually becomes uneasy and restless; moving about from place to place, scratching in corners or tearing up her bed and whimpering. At intervals she may stretch out at full length, have spells of panting and seem apprehensive. Examination will reveal that the vulva is swollen and there may be a thick, mucous discharge. The first puppy may be born within half an hour of these symptoms, or its arrival may be delayed for several hours. The duration of labour varies widely. It is often longer in a bitch having her first litter than in a matron. Parturition may be delayed by the absence of uterine contractions, or by their being too weak or infrequent to effect delivery. Uterine inertia is more common in untried bitches than in those which have previously been bred from. Bitches that are too fat or in soft condition are especially liable to suffer from this trouble.

If labour continues for longer than three hours without terminating in a birth, veterinary assistance should be sought. There may be an obstruction, such as an unusually large or an awkwardly placed puppy, which must be removed before parturition can proceed. As a rule, however, when the uterine contractions become sufficiently strong the young whelp in its fluid-filled envelope moves down from its position in one of the horns of the uterus, eventually reaching the orifice of the vagina. Usually the sac bursts or is ruptured by the bitch as the puppy is born. Normally a whelp comes head first, and once the head is through the body follows easily and quickly. Sometimes, however, the youngster emerges tail-end first. In either case, little if any assistance may be needed beyond easing the shoulders through or correcting the position of a hind limb which is impeding delivery. The membranes ensheathing the new born puppy will be torn away by the bitch. She will then bite through the umbilical cord and proceed to lick the youngster, rolling it about to dry and stimulate it.

The afterbirth, consisting of the placenta and the remains of the foetal membranes, should be voided about a quarter of an hour after a birth and will probably be promptly swallowed by the bitch. It is most important to see that all the afterbirths are expelled from the uterus before parturition is considered completed. If anything remains behind, complications—which may be fatal—may arise, so be sure to check the afterbirths and confirm that they correspond with the number of puppies born. If there is any doubt have the bitch examined by a veterinary surgeon within the next forty-eight hours.

When the first puppy has been born the rest of the litter may be expected to arrive at intervals of from half an hour to two hours. Some bitches deliver their offspring at pretty regular intervals, but others are most irregular, having two or three quickly then resting for a long time before producing any more. Most Whippet bitches are able to deal with a whelping unaided but it is always advisable to keep a careful though unobtrusive watch, so that should assistance be needed it may be immediately forthcoming. The great majority of the difficulties which crop up may be easily dealt with by a watchful observer, but if help is not at hand at the right moment a valuable whelp or a whole litter may be lost. In a highly strung or timid bitch labour may be inhibited by a nervous or hysterical condition. Such a bitch should be attended, from the time she is expected to whelp until all her puppies have been safely born, by someone to whom she is attached. The aim must be to give her a feeling of confidence and security. At such a time the sound of a familiar voice will do more than anything else to overcome fear and prevent panic.

For the first few days after the birth of a litter the motions of the bitch will be loose and black. This is quite normal, but should black diarrhoea persist beyond the fourth day a small dose of castor oil may be given. A red discharge from the vagina may be expected to continue in decreasing volume for from three to seven days after parturition. If it shows signs of increasing unduly after the fourth day with a rise in temperature, uterine infection may be suspected and a veterinary surgeon should be consulted.

8

NURSING AND REARING PUPPIES

FOR THE FIRST two days after whelping the bitch should be kept on a very light diet. Liquids, such as thin gruel, cereals in milk, or egg beaten up in lukewarm milk, is all that is required at this time. On the third day broth may be given and crumbled or kibbled wholemeal rusk added to the milk foods. On the fourth day well-boiled fish, paunch or rabbit may be introduced and this diet continued for a further two days. This method of feeding will provide all the nourishment needed by the bitch, help to keep her temperature down and guard against digestive upsets, which are very likely to occur if the stomach is over-loaded. The feeding of raw meat and other solids at this time will encourage stimulation of the milk glands before the puppies are vigorous enough to cope with the flow, and that may result in the formation of breast abscesses. By the end of the week the youngsters should be feeding lustily and be able to take all the milk produced. From then on the feeding of the dam must be generous and include raw and cooked meat, eggs, milk and wholemeal cereals plus a daily dose of fish-liver oil and a mineral supplement. In fact, at this stage the bitch cannot be done too well, providing she is given adequate exercise to keep her hard and fit. It is, however, important to realize that heavy feeding too soon after whelping is fraught with danger both to the bitch herself and her puppies.

Weaning
For the first three weeks of their lives the dam should provide all the food needed by the puppies, but at the end of that time, if all has gone well, the milk teeth will be piercing the gums and the youngsters may be taught to lap. The best liquid food to begin with is egg and milk mixture, prepared by beating the yolk of an egg in half a pint of full-cream milk, or one of the powder milk preparations put up for kennel use. The food should be given at

blood heat, a little being poured into a saucer and placed before a puppy. He will probably sniff at it and get a drop or two on his nose or lips. This will be licked and once the taste has registered he will be eager for more. If there is any difficulty, gently press the puppy's nose into the saucer. At first this may cause some spluttering or sneezing, but with a little perseverance the baby will try tentatively to lap. Some puppies learn more quickly than others, but if the lesson is repeated daily, all will be lapping well within a few days.

At the same age they may have their first taste of raw, lean meat. This must be finely scraped—not minced—and be free from gristle or other hard particles. A Whippet puppy should be given about as much as will roll up into a ball the size of a marble, or a small teaspoonful. Nearly all youngsters take to this greedily, but the meat ration must not be overdone at first. One feed a day is sufficient, but after a week or ten days two may be given. If a puppy is allowed to stuff itself with too much scraped meat, as it will try to do, its digestion is likely to suffer, causing it to lose its appetite for the dam's milk and producing distended stomach, dehydration and irregular bowel action. But if the quantity of meat is reasonably restricted and increased very gradually to keep pace with growth and development, no set-backs will occur.

By the time the puppies are five or six week old they should be having four supplementary meals daily in addition to what they may be obtaining from their dam. From the sixth week Farex, crumbled wholemeal rusks or fine biscuit meal may be added to one of the milk feeds, or given with good broth from which all fat has been removed, or with raw egg, and the number of the meals increased to five. That number should be maintained until about the end of the tenth week, when one feed may be dropped. If weaning is made a gradual process, by beginning supplementary feeding at about three weeks, the change over from mother's milk to solid food and a more varied diet may be effected without any trouble and without causing distress either to the puppies or their dam.

The amount of food offered must, of course, depend on the size,

Opposite: Ch. Crysbel Skylark with her litter (Photo: Anne Cumbers).

appetite and nutritional needs of the individual youngster, but no more should be given at a meal than is eaten readily without unduly distending the stomach. A puppy should be well fed and look plumpish, but overloading the digestive organs with bulky, starchy foods must be avoided. If the growing body becomes too fat, it may be too heavy for the immature limbs to support and result in faulty shoulders, pasterns and quarters, making the dog unsound for life. If a puppy tends to lose weight or condition after weaning, it may generally be put right by daily doses of Parrish's Food, Radiomalt or Virol. All are fine conditioners and will do much to help a poor doer or improve an indifferent appetite.

Diet

While it would be wrong to suggest that the feeding of growing youngsters must follow a set pattern, the following is offered as a suitable menu on which the diet of an eight-weeks' old Whippet puppy may be based:

First meal: Egg and milk mixture, or other milk food, with cereal, crumbled wholemeal rusk or fine biscuit meal.

Second meal: Minced lean meat, liver, tripe or fish, with stale wholemeal bread crumbs. The whole moistened with good stock or gravy.

Third meal: Milk food thickened with Farex, oatmeal or other cereal.

Fourth meal: Raw meat or egg mixed with wholemeal crumbs or soaked kibbled rusks.

Fifth meal: Milk food.

Meat or its equivalent in protein value should account for from half to two thirds of the weight of food given. From the fifth week until the puppies are twelve months old each should have a daily dose of fish-liver oil and calcium. If wholemeal rusks and meal are used there should be no need to provide additional vitamin B, but yeast tablets are useful in keeping skin and coat in good condition and in preventing teething troubles.

Opposite: Whippet puppies enjoying their meat feed (Photo: Anne Cumbers).

As the puppies grow their food should include less liquid. The meat may be coarsely minced, then cut into small pieces. The cereal ingredients may be fed moist or dry. Sloppy food should be avoided as soon as more solid fare can be dealt with. At six months a puppy may be ready to go on to the adult diet of two meals daily, except that fish-liver oil and calcium must be continued until growth is completed. A dish of egg and milk may be offered in the early morning or at night, in addition to the solid meals, to a slow developer or to a youngster which is short of condition.

Health and hygiene

Among the chief anxieties concerning the rearing of puppies are those relating to the possible impact of disease and how to keep them growing steadily and developing satisfactorily. Wise feeding can do much to ward off or minimize the effects of illness and ensure normal development and soundness. Bad rearing or indifferent feeding are not always the direct cause of structural defects, unsoundness or bad movement, but they can cause loss of stamina, stunted growth, lightness of bone or muscular weakness, all of which may adversely affect movement and in extreme cases may be responsible for very obvious unsoundness.

Because of their susceptibility to infection, it is advisable to keep young puppies away from other dogs and to prevent their being handled by strangers. After a youngster has been inoculated against para-distemper, hepatitis and the leptospiral diseases, at about ten weeks; such precautions are not so important, but early in puppyhood every possible effort should be made to reduce the risk of infection to a minimum.

In the successful rearing of puppies it is impossible to over estimate the importance of scrupulous attention to hygiene. Many of the disease-producing germs that enter the body may be passed in the urine or faeces. The greatest care should be taken to prevent puppies having access to their own or the dam's excreta. Remember that germs flourish in a stuffy, moist atmosphere and that, though warmth and freedom from draught are essential, it is most necessary to see that the puppy quarters are quite dry and sufficiently ventilated to enable fresh air to circulate freely. All utensils used for the preparation and serving of food must be kept absolutely clean and meat stored in a cool place away from possible contamination by flies.

When they are strong on their legs puppies should have access to the open air and be furnished with ample opportunities to romp and play while enjoying unrestricted freedom. A warm, dry bed to which they may retire when tired must always be provided. Young puppies should sleep at frequent intervals and rest after a meal is especially beneficial. If a romp precedes a meal the food will be consumed with relish, and the full-fed youngster be ready to rest quietly in its sleeping box for a time; but if shut up in a small kennel through the day it will become bored and fretful, soon losing condition and appetite. Constant close confinement is very bad for Whippet puppies. It makes them nervous, lethargic and stupid, besides being a frequent cause of unsoundness.

The permanent teeth, which replace the milk dentition, usually start to erupt at between the third and the fourth month. As they grow the puppy teeth generally become loose and are shed. Occasionally, however, some of the first teeth are retained, so that the two sets are present together in the jaws. When that occurs the milk teeth must be drawn to enable the permanent teeth to occupy their correct positions. The permanent dentition is usually complete by the time a puppy is from five to six months old. Teething is materially assisted by providing a hard biscuit or suitable bone on which the puppy may chew two or three times a week.

All puppies should be wormed at the age of four or six weeks. Nearly all of them harbour round worms however carefully they may have been reared, and unless these internal parasites are got rid of at the time of weaning a puppy cannot thrive. Worming the bitch before mating or during the early stages of pregnancy will help to ensure a less wormy puppy.

9

COLOUR BREEDING

ONE OF THE MANY attractions of the Whippet is the wide range of colours found in the breed, so that one may find a dog of almost any colour to suit one's own particular taste. Most Whippet lovers regard colour as of little moment, but a growing number of people seem to be eager to be able to forecast with some degree of certainty just which colours may be expected from specific matings. The subject of colour breeding in the Whippet is somewhat complicated and to understand it clearly it is necessary to grasp certain basic principles of genetics.

Dominant characteristics
The first essential is to have a clear understanding of what is meant by the terms 'dominant' and 'recessive' as applied to hereditary characteristics. When we refer to a colour as being dominant to another we mean that if genes for both are present in the same individual only the dominant colour will be shown, the other, the recessive, being masked or hidden. It is only when recessive genes come together in duplicate—that is when one is received from each of the parents—that a recessive colour will be visually expressed. An appreciation of the significance of these two terms is essential if the reason puppies in a litter bred from parents of a particular colour may not only differ among themselves in respect of colour but may be quite different from either of the parents, is to be understood. Another point which must be firmly grasped is that the quality of dominance has nothing to do with the frequency of persistence with which a colour crops up in a breed or strain.

This may be clearer if we take an example for consideration. If a brindle dog which is pure bred for its colour is mated to a fawn bitch, also pure bred for the colour she shows, all the resulting puppies will be brindle, because brindle is dominant to fawn. What actually happens is that the dog passes a gene, or hereditary unit, for brindle to each of his offspring, while the bitch passes a gene for fawn to each of hers. All their puppies will, therefore, carry one gene for each colour in their genetic make-up. But because the effect of the brindle-determining gene is dominant to that of the fawn-determining gene, the influence of the latter will be unapparent, so that in external appearance the puppies arising from the mating will be indistinguishable, so far as colour is concerned, from pure-bred brindles. But, despite their colour, each of the dogs so bred will, when mature, produce two types of germ cells, half of which will carry a brindle-determining gene and the other half a fawn-determining factor, so that if mated either to one another or to a fawn they must be expected to produce both brindle and fawn puppies. Though a fawn may be born from two brindle parents each of which carries fawn as a recessive, a brindle can never come from the mating of two fawns, since were either of the parents carrying the brindle gene that colour would be visually apparent.

In the Whippet the basic colours may be said to be brindle, fawn, white, black and a combination of those hues. Of these brindle is dominant to fawn and all other colours. Fawn is dominant to black. Whole colour is imperfectly dominant to particolour, that is to say that, though the progeny resulting from the mating of a whole colour to a particolour may resemble its whole coloured parent most strongly, it will probably show the influence of its other parent in the shape of white markings on feet, chest, muzzle or elsewhere. In other cases, too, slight differences may sometimes be detected between individuals which are genetically pure for a dominant colour and those which are impure, though at first sight both may look the same. For instance, a fawn Whippet mated to a black will have fawn puppies (fawn being the dominant colour), but close examination may reveal a number of black or black-tipped hairs distributed through the coat, possibly with a black mask.

Modifiers
The visual expression of a main gene may be influenced by the presence of secondary genes or modifiers. Such secondary genes may have a paleing or a deepening effect on coat colour. This is well shown in the Whippet, in which brindle may vary from dark

to light, with the striping showing a blackish, red, fawn, silver or blue ground colour beneath. Then there is the dilution factor which converts black into blue. Where two colours appear together on the same animal the dilution factor will affect both, so that a red coat with black shadings and mask will be changed by the action of dilution genes to blue fawn with a bluish mask, or a golden brindle to blue or grey brindle. Modifying and diluting genes are recessive to genes for the development of full colour, so that while puppies of the paler shades may be bred from full coloured parents, two animals showing dilute pigmentation cannot produce fully pigmented progeny.

Inhibiting factors

So far nothing has been said about the white Whippet. That is because this colour is, genetically, not what it appears to be! The white Whippet seen at our shows is not an albino—which is an animal incapable of forming pigment in any part of the body—for the eyes are pigmented, as are often the nose and lips. A white dog of this kind carries latent colour. The reason it is white is that the hair follicles do not form pigment because of inhibiting factors. We must, in fact, consider the dog as being particoloured, but the visual colour is restricted to certain small areas, such as the eyes, nose etc.

A white Whippet may carry genes for any colour, whether black, fawn or brindle. It may also carry the dilution factor or genes either for a whole coloured or a patterned coat. In particolours the size, number and distribution of the coloured patches are controlled by the interaction of various ancillary genes, so that it is virtually impossible to stabilize any specific shape of marking, but the colour shown by the patches follows the same method of inheritance as it does in the whole coloured coat. That is to say, that brindle markings are dominant to fawn, fawn to black and black to blue.

The presence of the colour inhibiting factor which occurs in all white dogs may cause very unexpected results in breeding. If, for example, a white carrying latent fawn or a fawn particolour is mated to a black, the puppies will carry the inhibiting gene transmitted by the white or particoloured parent, and the gene for whole black colour inherited from the other. As fawn is dominant to black and the whole coloured coat imperfectly dominant to the particolour pattern, the puppies may be expected to be solid fawns with some white on feet, chest etc. But all will, provided both their parents are genetically pure for their respective colours, carry genes for black and for their particolour pattern. If, on the other hand, the sire was white carrying latent brindle and the dam fawn, the puppies would be brindle, though that colour was not shown by either parent.

Problems of colour inheritance

These brief particulars of the laws which apply to colour inheritance in the Whippet may enable the reader to understand how it is that in this breed litters so often include puppies of several different colours, and why a dog or bitch of a particular colour may never have a single son or daughter of that colour. In the Standard it is expressly stated that colour is of no importance, and as a result the interbreeding of the various colours has gone on haphazard for innumerable generations. This has been responsible for the virtual absence of genetic purity in respect of colour throughout the breed, so that, save in a few exceptional cases, it is impossible to forecast with certainty the colours the puppies born from any mating will show. In a brindle to fawn mating, for example, either the sire or the dam, or both, may carry black, particolour, white or the dilution factor, so that the colours included in the litter will vary according to how the recessive or dominant genes happen to come together in the fertilized ova from which the individual puppies develop.

Another thing which has a very important bearing on the problems presented by colour inheritance, is the fact that litter brothers or sisters may be quite different genetically regarding colour, even though they may both have coats of the same shade. To make this clear let us consider the mating of a white dog carrying latent fawn to a black bitch carrying the dilution factor. The resulting puppies will be fawn or fawn with some white. If two members of this litter are bred together their offspring may be expected to include fawns, blue fawns, blacks and blues, most of the whole colours being more or less marked with white. But some

C

of the fawns will carry genes for black and/or the dilution factor, while others of the same colour will not. Similarly, the blacks produced may or may not carry the dilution factor. If mated to blues the former will throw blue as well as black puppies, whereas the latter will throw only blacks.

Blacks and blues

Black has never been a common colour in the show Whippet, though it was often seen in the old racing dog. This colour has attracted the attention of several breeders recently, who have been fascinated by the problems met with in efforts to breed one particular colour. In this regard the names of Mrs. Martin, Mrs. M. B. Garrish, Mr. Pat Salter and the late Mrs. W. M. Wigg must be specially mentioned, for they more than any others have devoted much time and thought to the production of high-class Whippets of this colour.

The idea that black is difficult to breed and when obtained is hard to perpetuate, doubtless arises from the fact that it acts as recessive to the more common colours, like brindle and fawn. Being recessive it can only be shown by a dog which carries the gene for its development in duplicate. This means that a black Whippet can only be bred if that colour appears on both sides of its pedigree. Thus, the mating of a black dog with a fawn bitch will (unless the fawn carries the factor for black as a recessive) produce no blacks at all, no matter how often the mating is repeated. But a black masked red mated either to a bitch of his own colour or to a brindle, fawn or particolour carrying black may be expected to sire a proportion of black puppies.

As has been mentioned, blue is closely related to black, being the effect of a double dose of the dilution factor acting on black pigmentation. As it is recessive to black, the mating of blue and black will give a whole litter of blacks unless, of course, the black parent carries a single gene for blue, in which case blacks and blues may be expected to arrive in about equal numbers.

It is important to understand that it does not matter at all

Opposite: The black Whippets Ebzan Noudini Bey-Noir (right) and his son Chancerick Kaloson (left) descended from the late Mrs Wigg's colour line.

whether the gene for a recessive colour was introduced within the last generation or by a distant ancestor. The essential point is that the gene must be carried by both parents. Recently a breeder was very much surprised to obtain in a litter of eight, bred from a fawn to blue mating, six blue and two black puppies, though the sire was known to have been fawn bred for five generations. But the fact that black and blue puppies were sired by this dog proves conclusively that he carries the gene for black and the dilution factor as recessives despite the circumstance that for five generations his ancestors have been visual fawns. It might be necessary to go back far beyond the limits of his known pedigree to trace the ancestor through which these factors were introduced. The breeding result mentioned makes it quite certain that the genes have been transmitted along this line and retained in this particular dog.

Because breeders have so often mixed black with other colours in breeding, comparatively few blacks are bred, even by those who specially want them. There have only been three champions of this colour in the breed to date, these being Ch. Poppy Tarquin, Ch. Black Diamond of Annalyn and Ch. Ladiesfield Starturn, the last named probably the best Whippet dog of the colour yet seen. We have yet to see a 'blue' champion—the only dog of this colour to get a Challenge Certificate was Blue Streak in the early 1950s. Boughton Blue Beau (bred and exported by Miss M. Boggia) was made an International Champion on the continent.

Breeding for true colour
To stabilize any colour within a strain so that it becomes true breeding, a consistent programme of inbreeding and selection must be pursued. This involves a very real element of danger, in that in striving for colour, which, it must again be stressed, is not recognised by the Standard as having any significance compared with type and structural soundness, other qualities of essential importance are apt to be sacrificed. It is not inevitable that this should be so, but breeders who are tempted to concentrate on building up a kennel of Whippets of a particular colour must be very careful to keep this danger in mind and to retain a sense of proportion when arranging matings.